D0841027

To Mary
with blessings and love,
May you always hear
the Spirit.
Ella

"I'm Right Here"

(Mornings With My Higher Power)

by
Ella Jankowiak

authorHOUSE®

AuthorHouse™
1663 Liberty Drive, Suite 200
Bloomington, IN 47403
www.authorhouse.com
Phone: 1-800-839-8640

First published by AuthorHouse 11/28/2007

ISBN: 978-1-4343-2647-8 (sc)

Cover Design by Christine Bogdan

*Printed in the United States of America
Bloomington, Indiana*

This book is printed on acid-free paper.

This book is dedicated to the spirit within each
of you that is waiting to be heard.

"I'm Right Here"

(Mornings With My Higher Power)

Ella Jankowiak

"Speak to Him then for He hears,
And Spirit with Spirit can meet...
Closer is He than breathing
And nearer than hands and feet."
-Alfred, Lord Tennyson

Introduction

My spiritual journey began thirty years ago. As a wife and mother of three, with a small home-based business, I wanted to start my days with prayer. But I usually experienced hectic mornings when my prayer time was interrupted by phone calls, packing lunches and finding lost items. Then other seemingly urgent chores distracted me and I would never find my way back to my prayers once I was pulled away. I wanted connection to God to be a priority so I began to pray in the form of a letter to God. In this way, I was able to capture my thoughts easier and express my feelings with more clarity. This also enabled me to stop and start again without feeling that I had lost my train of thought.

As words tumbled onto the page, old memories floated to the surface, things I had long buried and thought I had forgotten. Tears of anger or sorrow often slid from my eyes and I sometimes had to stop and wait until I could see again to continue. Feeling the feelings, blowing my nose, wiping the tears, and creating mounds of tissues around me, I journeyed into my soul.

Other wonderful memories came back too. I rejoiced in the love and happiness that I remembered. I began to see a balance to my life, a beauty and a perfection that I never realized had existed.

But usually my prayers took the form of worrying

about a person or situation that I had judged to be a problem. I urged God to zap the person into shape or rearrange the situation to suit me.

I also found I was whining about things I actually could do something about but was in fact too lazy or afraid to try. This happened a lot. I played the victim to the limit.

One morning I was especially stressed. I wanted God to be here and now. I needed comfort and encouragement that I could actually feel. I was sinking into a dark fear that maybe I was wasting my time. I cried, "God, help me. Where are you?"

In the depth of my soul a voice answered: "I'm right here. Be still long enough to listen."

I was astounded by the reality of that experience. I could no longer deny that someone, or something was actually listening to me. Was it really God?

I continued my morning letters and soon I began to notice a tug to write down what seemed to be the answer to that particular problem. It was as if someone was dictating to me and so I began to let the words come. I wrote in pencil in large, spiral notebooks. In the beginning I was uncomfortable to think I was actually getting a message from God. It must be only my imagination. This couldn't really be happening. But it seemed I could not stop it and I could not explain it.

In fact, the writings were often quite blunt and to the point. They gave me the wisdom that I needed and the strength to keep going. They were also gentle, comforting and loving. On days that I had no time to write, I could open the book at almost any page and find that the answer would help me with whatever problem was currently filling my mind.

The answers were quite short at first, but as I began to trust, I found that God had a lot to say. I am still in awe of this whole experience and yet often I am still unwilling to follow the suggestions that I am privileged to write. So many seem to repeat themselves but I have found that only by repetition do I really get it. Even then, I usually choose to "forget" the way to peace.

One of the most difficult decisions has been that I share these answers with others. I have only done it a few times with one or two specific letters that I thought would comfort someone. The people I read them to usually wanted a copy so they could read it over again. Several friends suggested I put them in the form of a book. I have been very hesitant to do this. Who was I to say that God was speaking to me? What would I do if others judged me? I wasn't sure I would have the courage to risk criticism or ridicule. I told myself that I would do it when I had more time.

Because of my fear and apprehension, I kept myself busy with anything that would not allow time for this book. God, however, had other plans. My business phone almost totally stopped ringing. I have had blocks of free time presented to me that I could not ignore. No amount of shopping, napping or eating has managed to get me off the hook. And so I begin to share with you this intimate journey that has allowed my soul to grow and change and heal because of these amazing answers.

The prayers I wrote and the questions I asked are not important. In fact, they would probably distract you from applying the answers to your particular situation. What is it that you want to hear from that seemingly elusive God you turn to? There is no power failure. You are always connected to your source. Be willing to be still long enough to hear the small, still voice that whispers to your soul. Try to suspend your disbelief for a little while and remember a time when anything was possible. It still is!

Beginnings

eginnings can be both exciting and scary. This is the beginning of an amazing adventure. You are not alone. I am always, all ways with you, as close as your breath is to your body. I love you. I know your fears, your deepest needs. Trust that I am working out a perfect plan for your life. I have many new things to show you. But for now, before you begin your day, go outside for awhile and listen to the music of my world. Hear the melody, changing but ever present. The seasons, colors, scents, sounds will shift and ebb, but always continue. Choose to see me there; my rhythm and my mystery. Soon you will feel the rhythm and my ways will no longer be mysterious. I am here within and without, in wood grain and sunlight, in water and sound, in breath and in tears. I want to share myself with you, to help you find your joy. Begin today to view the world in a new and exciting way. This is a journey of the spirit.

Joy

You are ready to begin a new phase of our relationship. You will know me better. I want to use you, your pain and your joy, to reach others. Show them both sides of your coin. It will purchase peace for them. I will lead you where you need to go. Your message is not words, but joy. Words are cheap and many spend them foolishly. They speak of loving me and then hate each other, they talk of my power then wallow in despair, they tell of my grace and then worry themselves sick, they say I am reliable but then do not trust me. Be what I need; not words but *action*, not preaching my joy but *living* it. I will be with you, guiding, loving, blessing your efforts. Nothing is too small, no one is insignificant.

The Key

I know you are struggling with a relationship. Listen to me, there is no real conflict. I have not asked you to be a slave to another or lose your dignity. There will be times you can joyfully submit, and times you can joyfully challenge. But joyfully is the key, wholeheartedly is the answer. Don't agree and then drag your feet. Give your all. Stop playing games. I have given you this person as a gift. You need them to grow and develop just as they need you. There are no accidents. You will know what you need to do if you ask me to help you. Joy is your key, joy and enthusiasm in your work and your life. If you use this key, it will unlock many doors.

Plans

My child, take time each day for these three things: seek me within your heart, release your confusion by committing your day to a written plan, then do first what you wish to do least. I am watching and helping you. You are not alone. My strength is available to you, my peace is within your reach. I know your heart. Your plans may fall through but remember that your ultimate goal is me. I am your source and your destination. Your life situation is only the path you have chosen this time. You are where you are due to decisions you have made. Seek me in your work, your family, your personal contacts. I am present in the least endeavor, the smallest thought. Do not confuse the details of your life with the ultimate yearnings of your heart. You long for peace and happiness, you ache for understanding. In time you will be healed of your pain and fear. They will disappear back into the no-thing that they are. Do not focus on them. Lean on me. I will lift you over your fears with my love.

Presence

My child, you need to remember my power is great. Ask me moment to moment to guide and direct your actions, renew your feeble energy and inspire your thoughts. When you do a task, do it for me. My presence is there always. That cup you wash is mine, that gift you buy is for me, the love you show is to me. I am there with you, in the people you see and the sounds you hear. In the freshness of morning and the weariness of night. Look for me. I will renew, inspire and redirect you. Listen for me. I speak in the stillness to your heart. Peace and order will flow from you like music when you tune yourself to me.

Mind and Body

*D*on't let your body tell your mind how it must feel. Let your mind control your body. It is very powerful and truly does this anyway. You just do not realize it. The mind projects its fears onto your body and that is disease. Still your mind. Empty it of all its fantasy and let me fill it with truth. Quiet the chatter, make room in your mental clutter for new ideas. Breathe... Be still. Clarity will come to you. It takes time but it will change everything. Then you will have less need of "things" to remind you of who you are and what your purpose is. As easily and silently as sunrise you will begin to understand. The light will come and the path will be clear. You are wonderful, you are holy, you are eternal. Trust me to guide your mind.

God Everywhere

*W*hen choosing between a difficult and an easy way to travel, remember that the more difficult path will offer you more opportunities to grow and learn. My grace will guide you and will shine the brightest during the darkest hours. Before you, beside you, behind you, above, beneath and within you, I am. Just turn your head, I am there. Speak my name, I will hear. Think of my love, I will know. Your quest to find me is tiring you and you have become addicted to the search. I am already found. Open your mind, your ears, and your heart. Be still a while and you will come to know I am everywhere, everything, and everyone. When you open yourself to everything and everyone you will open yourself to me. That is where I live, in even the arrogant, the angry and afraid. You will find me there or not at all.

Answers

*S*top asking for answers that you already have. You know exactly what to do, you just do not want to do it. I know it is not easy but when you choose the better way I will offer you my strength. Here is the answer to any problem - turn to me instead. Instead of food, money, power, vanity, alcohol, drugs, control, thrills, things, instead of whatever stops your progress. Which one do you want to serve? At what altar do you worship? You have made a god of your wants and you sacrifice your life and self-worth to it. You have spoiled the child and tantrums will continue for awhile. But remember who is in charge here. There is no power in the world that can overcome my love but you can choose to turn away. I am Health, and Love and Life and I am here. Choose me.

The Path Home

Beloved, it matters not the path you take to home, the path is determined by where you are when you begin. All paths lead to me. There really is no other goal, only imagined ones. Some roads are very winding and even seem to lead away at times. There are turns and peaks and valleys. Some are more scenic and beautiful and others are more rough and difficult. The road that is lovely in springtime is often treacherous in winter. Remember only this when it appears you have lost your way: All roads lead home to me. You are my child and I will not let you wander far. I wait and watch for your return.

A Holy Place

This special place you love so much seems to be a holy place because you will it so. Each place you walk becomes in truth a sacred spot when you are there. It is because you bring your spirit there that it is blessed. Seek not external settings to receive my grace. You are the only thing I need to bless you. Begin to take this sense of holiness with you to all places, your home, your work, your play and you will find me already there before you, waiting with my arms open to comfort and to heal. There is no other place but here, there is no other time but now.

Not Your Problem

eloved, release your need to control others. It is unnecessary. You are fighting the wind. It will blow when and where it pleases and there are reasons for its movement which are hidden from your understanding. One day you will comprehend everything. But for now it is more important that you just control yourself. Isn't that a big enough task? Concern yourself with you and me. The rest is in my care.

Breathe

My peace is yours. Breathe in its gentleness, breathe out your worries and your fears. Breathe in my wisdom, my power, release your tension and your pain. Each breath you take becomes a time of grace if you so choose. Breathe in light, breathe out darkness, breathe in peace, exhale regret. Each step, each heartbeat then becomes a psalm of life instead of death, a melody of love in place of fear. The choice is yours. What do you wish to see and feel? Breathe in. . . . . . .

Your Guest

*D*ear one, offer this day to me, this hour, this minute, this breath and you will find the peace you seek. Conduct yourself as if I were with you - - I am. Prepare your house as if I were your guest - - I always have been. Try to feel my presence and soon you will know your search is over for I am already here. In everything you think and do and see, remember me.

Be Here Now

*B*e conscious, be aware. Bring your mind and spirit to this moment. Mindful awareness of my presence and this moment is a true meditation. So many wonderful experiences have been lost because you were absent to them. Bring yourself back to where you are and involve yourself with your life. Escape is an illusion and can become a trap. There is no need for it. Be with me in this holy instant and you will come to know my peace. I am here, do not run from my love. Now is truly all there is.

Quiet

Only when you quiet your mind, empty it of your planning and judging and fear, will there be room for me to enter. Hold on to nothing. This is your ego demanding to be heard. It will stop eventually. Create a holy place within your heart and soul. I will feel your welcome love and fill you with my truth.

Communion

Be still with me awhile. Sink down into the bliss of being one with me. Turn away for just a while from all the world's demands and just be still. This time of sweet communion will touch and bless all other things to which you bring your hands and mind. The more we join and share our love, the more love there will be to give away. This time is holy. Do not deny yourself this blessing. Remember who you are and why we need to spend some time together. Come to me and I will always, always hear you.

Work

The type of work you choose is not as important as the love with which you do it. Whatever you do will be right for you if you direct your heart and mind to choose love first. As you grow, you will choose more wisely. There is no wrong decision, only different ones. As always, I will help you if you let me.

Peace

How do you decide when to be at peace? Will it be when all your tasks are done? That will never be. Will it be when everyone else in your life is happy? You will wait forever. Perhaps when you have accomplished your goals. That will only be temporary because you will set others. Understand that your peace cannot depend on what is going on outside of you. It is an internal matter. There will always be external chaos. If your peace depends upon that, then you are a victim of the world. If you will come to me and tell me of your fears, together we will find a better way. I will not leave you. This is my prescription for peace.....I love you.

Temple Bell

All of your life is holy, even the difficult, uncomfortable moments. Believe in yourself and you will believe in me. I am in you, guiding and protecting your every action. I know this is hard to remember. Try to attach a common daily event to my presence. Perhaps the phone ringing could be your temple bell reminding you that all is well and I am here. Pause a fleeting moment before you pick up the call and think of me. The calls will be a blessing and you will extend that grace to all whose lives you touch.

Grace

Beloved, small are the sorrows you face. If you meet them with grace you will behold a gift there. Do you believe that I am with you and love you? Then act like it. It is no great thing to be joyful in the joyful times. But to be so in times of sadness, that is where you find the blessings. That is grace.

Past And Future

Your answer to your distress lies in this shining, holy moment. It is clean and beautiful unless you bring the past or future into it. Be joyful now! Be here now! This is the lesson: here and now is all there is. And I am always here, now.

Hide And Seek

*A*ll that is required is that you remember me. Recognize me in the one who stands before you. In spite of appearance, *I AM THERE!* Just see me and my holiness within them. In that instant you will be reborn to the awareness of truth. It does not matter what they say or do; they are only the hiding place I have chosen this time. It is a game of hide and seek we play. Only you have forgotten it is a game and believe you are alone. You are not! This is your game, you made the rules and you can change the outcome whenever you decide. Seek me and I will find you.

Experience The Problem

emember when you were in school and had to work through mathematics problems? If the teacher just gave you the answers without making you struggle with the process, you would have learned nothing. You needed to experience the problem. Sometimes you learned that there are several ways to arrive at the solution. Regardless of how you approached the task, the answer was the same. I am the answer to all the problems. However you reach me is all right. Your struggle is your education, your thoughts are your pencil, the paper is your life. Don't get lost in the problem, just learn. Rejoice that the answer is at hand. I will always be your solution.

Difficulties

How hard you work at something that is simple. It is only your belief in external appearances that makes things so difficult. Don't just think of me in certain places or times, come to me with every choice, hear my call in every voice, see me in everyone you meet. Make my presence manifest in your ordinary day and it will become glorious. All your pain comes from your judgment and your perception. You can shift your awareness in an instant, and everything will change. Nothing external will appear different but you will be at peace.

Honor The Moment

To be more present to where you are and what you are doing, you must honor the moment. This instant with its sights, sounds and feelings will never come again. This precise mixture of colors and light is like a single snowflake, unique, magical and fleeting, gone almost before you are aware that it began. It cannot be held or purchased. This is life. This instant, this instant, this instant. You and I are eternal, all else will pass away. Enjoy it now while you and the moment are here.

Stillness

You are learning more about waiting, trusting and listening. You will be guided if you are still enough to hear. Keep practicing so you learn to quiet your mind and heart. Only then can you hear me. I will enter silently and whisper to your soul. You are surrounded by the stillness of heaven. Before you ask, I will answer. I am your guide, your teacher and your friend. I will not, cannot fail you. Believe.

Surrender

How long will you continue to struggle for the ego's goals? You think you can control the world and others when you fail to even control yourself. Begin now, today, to finally, completely surrender. Stop the battle. The ego thrives on war and only grows stronger. Until you surrender you will continue to be a victim of your own mind. The little, meaningless conflicts will go on and on. Surrender is not defeat, it is victory! You will give up only to win. When you think you are falling back, you will be relaxing into my embrace and I will never let you fall.

Expectations

I know your heart is heavy at times when another does not meet your expectations. Remember that there are many times that you do not meet theirs. Keep in mind that all of you will fail each other frequently. Your job is only to forgive and to accept forgiveness. Judging is better left to one more qualified. And when you are troubled in ways you cannot understand, return your thoughts to me. Remember my words, ask for my wisdom, feel my arms of love surround you. We will walk together through the pain. It is only temporary as is everything, except my love.

The Path To God

*Y*ou can come to me for anything and in many ways. These written words are just a form you have found that works for you. You love words and books, so that is how I can best reach your heart. Another might find my message in music, order, the growth of a child or a plant. I am not limited to words, I speak to hearts. Each one will find the way to hear me that serves them best. If anyone believes, and will try, I will come to them in their thoughts, their hearts, their daily struggles. I am the peace that each soul seeks. I am what they yearn for while they blindly pursue success, financial security, or approval of others. They are trying to squeeze water from a stone while I run clear and cool within their reach. Seek me first and all else will follow.

Spring

Extend yourself in softness and love to those near you. Notice how you feel when spring touches your senses. Be a springtime in another's winter. Bring hope, warmth and enthusiasm into a barren, cold heart. Even the branch that seems dead has in its core a spark of life. It will revive and bloom in the sunshine of your joy.

Music

Relax, but be aware. You can release your anxiety and still be fully tuned to the rhythm of your life. Your music is not the same as even those close to you. The notes and beats are what makes the song beautiful. Continue to seek the special tone that is yours alone. This will enhance the other notes in your life. Do not seek to imitate others at either end of the scale. Your music was written with you alone in mind in order for there to be harmony. I will help you. I write the song, I play the music, it is a song of love.

The Source

You are my hands and my voice to a lonely soul. Tell them of my love for them. Speak freely of my peace and joy. You have lived it so you have credibility now. I have shown you my power and you have seen your own weakness turn to strength. Rely on me to guide you, to send to you the ones that need your touch. I only use others - speakers, books, music, to help people understand. Hear the speaker, read the book, listen to the music, but know that everything comes from me and all is love.

God's Presence

Beloved, how would you behave if you were in the presence of God? Well, you are! Feel your heart beat, I am that close to you. I dwell in your soul, your thoughts, your dreams. I know your senses deceive you, your logic tells you this can't be. But it is true. I surround you. I am your child, your spouse, your work. I am the person on the phone, the driver of the other car. I am the glue that holds the universe together and I am stuck on you.

Resentment

When you release the person you resent you will feel better. They are who they choose to be. That is right for them. Let them be and enjoy what you can about them. Do you resent a tree for shading you from the sun, for dropping its leaves in your yard? That is its nature. The shade has a purpose, as do the falling leaves. Your resenting won't change it one bit. Fighting is like resisting the tide. It is impossible. Just know that the tide is coming and build your castles of sand a bit further back from the edge of the sea so they won't be swept away with the first wave. Know that the waves will come. Wishing, praying, crying won't stop them. This is part of growing up. Only a child keeps building his castles where the tide will wipe them out and keeps crying about it. You could build your's further from the waves, on a rock. Let me be your rock and build your castle of stronger stuff than sand. Of course that will be more work, but what do you really want? I will always be here waiting. Let me be your foundation, the rock that never fails.

Relationships

hat person you are concerned about is your own personal challenge, and will be your path to peace. The pain you feel is because you are trying to change them. Leave them alone. Their feelings are their own and you are not responsible for them. If they choose anger, for any reason, that is their choice. It has its seed within them. They may choose to let it grow instead of plucking it out. But they are the master of their own garden. With this in mind, see that you also are making the choice to let anxious feelings grow. You don't have to let them choke the flowers of joy in your own garden. They are like weeds that kill the beauty. It is easy to stop them while they are small. If you let their roots go deep, if just one seed escapes your notice, you will find them hard to eliminate. Remember how a gardener cares for his flowers, waters and nourishes the beautiful ones; prunes and uproots the ugly, unwanted ones. You are each the caretakers of your own internal gardens.

Sharing

My beloved child, you are growing and seeing my hand at work in your life, yet I still sense a yearning within you for material things. Don't confuse external trappings for internal substance. I am with you. That is your greatest treasure. Do not be afraid to share me with others. Speak to them of your inner world, of how we touch each others hearts. This gift is available to them too. If they believe, I will come to them in their thoughts, their dreams, their writing, their daily struggles. I am always here, loving and leading you home.

Confusion

You are feeling more confusion lately. That is because you are getting closer to the truth of your life. Your old nature wants to cling to the childish traits of irresponsibility and selfishness. The old habits die very slowly and seem to spring to life again from time to time. Do not despair, you can control the now. Do not lose sight of present moment power. Ask for my strength and my wisdom. My spirit can overcome all human weakness and I am always here.

Flight

My precious one, you do not yet truly trust me to provide for you. You are like the baby bird safe in its nest. You see others flying around you. You flap your wings and pretend to fly. But until you step out in thin air with your wings outstretched, trusting the air beneath them to support and lift you, you are still imprisoned in your nest. You are still a bird but only in flight do you find and fulfill your true potential. A bird that does not soar, for whatever reason, might as well be any earth-bound creature. You are mine, chosen by me to love and to extend my love to the world. Yet your wings are still untried. I have prepared your heart for flight. Believe me. You are able to rise above the fear of earthly matters. I am the lift that will break the bonds of earth. Fly high!

Approval

As you seek you will find. Keep laughter in your heart. You are still looking for approval from others. You only need it from yourself. You have always had it from me. When you were in your darkest hour and your deepest pain, I was with you. When you felt lost and confused, I was there. It is only when you refuse to trust me that you feel alone. I tell you this truth: all you need, all you seek is already within your grasp. It is waiting to be discovered.

New Eyes

*Y*ou will see even more as time goes on because you are learning how to look for what is already there. When you come from darkness into light your vision is limited, even painful for a while. As you adjust to the light, things often look harsh, not soft and shadowy as they did in the darkness. Old familiar objects are strangely new, their imperfections revealed and their beauty enhanced. And things that seemed spooky and frightening are shown for what they really are. The monsters of the darkness become friendly, comforting trusted friends that will aid you in your journey in this bright new day. You will see farther as well as clearer. Realize that you do not need to have new circumstances, you only need to come out of the darkness and see with new eyes.

Time

*Y*ou are on a journey of discovery. Sometimes your faith will be tested. These moments of quiet you share with me will become even more precious to you. Life sometimes turns around and surprises when it is least expected. Do not forsake our time together. Come to me and I will wrap a blanket of my love and strength around your broken heart. I will comfort and heal all your pain. It will seem like it takes a long time by your standards, but I have time in my very hands. This is what time was made for.

Action

Remember how you have seen another person struggle in the past and when they asked for advice you told them the steps they could take that would help relieve the situation? Then they seemed to disregard your words and continue on as usual. Well, you know I have already given you the answers you have asked for many times. Instead of more insight you need more action. Stop reading and talking so much and do the work that you say needs to be done. Your life is in your hands but you do not walk alone.

Like A River

*D*o you know the difference between what you think you should do and what truly needs doing? Relax in the beginning of a stress-building thought and realize the choices you have. Renew yourself with my love. Speak softly and slow your actions for a moment. Consult your inner voice, my voice. It will seem like a new idea that springs up out of barren ground. Let that thought bubble in your mind for a while to refresh you, then follow it as it runs pure and clear in the sunlight. It is the beginning of change, like the birth of a river that gives all it touches life and growth. Flow with it and in time, like a river it will carry you.

Seeds Of Peace

The peace you are beginning to experience is a gift you have given to yourself. You have begun to realize that I do not give or take, reward or punish. I am a coexister in your life. The world should neither bless or curse me for its triumphs or its tragedies. I am the comforter of the inner world. Deep inside your heart is my domain but that too is up to you to let me in. I do not force myself on anyone. I am available for everyone to gain strength and peace but the choice is always theirs. Some are more ready than others. Just keep planting seeds for me. I remember where you have dropped them. Sometimes it takes many tears to soften a hard heart and prepare it so my roots of peace can go down deep. You are only the seed sower. You are not responsible for the growth. That job belongs to me. Do your part and I will always do mine.

Brightness

There is a flame of light within you that is me. You and I are one. You only need to love and understand yourself more and you will know more of me. You are life and light, warmth and radiance, enthusiasm and joy. Do not darken your brightness with thoughts of fear or failure, sorrow or pain, anger or guilt. Shine brightly with my energy and let the light that you hold bring peace and healing wherever you are. You carry the flame of love in you and so does everyone, but most do not let their light shine. You are my gift to the ones still in darkness. Like one candle bringing its light to another, let the fire of my love be passed on. I am here beside you, the keeper of your flame.

Progress

*D*ear one, do not equate your progress by measuring your pain. That will result in feelings of failure. There will always be some pain in your earthly life, especially if you continually search for it. But the good news is that you now have the choice to focus instead on your peace. You have a new point of view when you look at life through my eyes. Do not measure your spirit by the world's standards. That is like trying to contain water in a basket or helium in a cup. Trust me to measure your love and humility, your faith and your kindness in the light that sees your heart and not the darkness that hides it. You are on the right path, I walk beside you.

Wisdom

*Y*ou will never truly hear me until you give up your version of what is right or wrong. Your judgment about a situation is what causes your pain. Let me be the judge and you turn your energy to other things, joy perhaps, loving is good too. Relinquishment of judgment is the beginning of wisdom. Choose peace instead.

Ego

Hold on to nothing. What you are clinging to is only your ego demanding to be heard. It will be quiet eventually. No matter what seems to be happening only love is real. Whenever you feel called to attack or defend you are choosing fear and that will never give you the peace you seek. Put aside your ego and choose love. That will never fail.

This Instant

To be more present to where you are and what you are doing, you must honor the moment. This means to bring your full attention to the task at hand. Are you making the bed, washing a dish, or reading the paper? Wherever you are, whatever you are doing is holy. How many times have hours slipped by and you were unaware of what you were doing? Those lost moments are precious. Begin today to treasure every instant with the same love with which I treasure you.

Let Go

*S*truggling pulls the knots tighter. You need to let go. Let go of projection and judgment, of old resentments and future outcomes. Be still in this moment and I will come to you in your quietness. Hold on to nothing. Remember who you are and why you are here. Your goal is today. Make this the best and most blessed now that you can. Show love, patience and forgiveness as much as you are able. Leave your tomorrows to me. I have never failed you. Be still long enough to hear me whisper to your heart. I am with you, closer than your breath, closer than your thoughts. Your stillness opens the door to your soul. I dwell within.

Motivation

Think about how motivated you can be when it is called for. Cleaning when company is coming, patience with a stranger, rising early for a trip. You can do all these things on any given day, the only difference is in your mind. You have the power but you must make the choice. I cannot do that for you. But if you remember who you really are, you will be more able to choose wisely. You are a child of God, spirit of the wind, you are myself in disguise, just as are all others. You need not cry or worry. You are guided, protected and loved.

Distress

*A*re you in distress? The dream always seems real when you are in it. The play you watch seems like truth if you really live the part. This is your drama. Of course to really explain and understand it while you are in it is almost impossible. A child in first grade struggles with his lessons. He cannot see how they are preparing him for second grade. He only experiences his own current frustration. And nowhere in his young mind is he able to conceive the idea that what he is doing now and how he is dealing with his small problems is preparing him for high school, college or life in general. Even if you were to explain it to him, he would just have a vague understanding. Only when he looks back from a higher place can he understand that everything he went through brought him to where he is. Maturity in life and spirit will be the only way you can understand. One day you will look back and comprehend the plan.

Turn It Over

Whatever worries you, whatever keeps you from joy, turn it over to me. All your worries are nothing but wasted energy. Your ego needs to control, the spirit wants to let go. Let go of your desire to have certain results. Whatever results you get, don't judge them as good or bad. They are what they are. How much does your worrying affect the outcome of anything? It is only a mind game you are playing. You think you are powerful enough to change things. You are only able to change yourself and you know how difficult that is. Your job in every situation is to do your best and then witness my power. Don't get caught up in your need to "fix" problems. You don't even know what the real problem is. You don't have to fix anything. In truth, you cannot. Come to me, the fixer of the real problem. You are safe, you are eternal, you are home.

Your True Self

How much I love you. How dear you are to me. I have my hand on your shoulder and my guidance is sure. Your physical self is not who you are. You are a being of light and love so immense and wonderful that your human mind cannot begin to comprehend it. You are wondrous and beautiful and ancient and wise. You are eternal and never-ending. You are peace and joy. It is just your present container that is limited. All your pain is due to that confinement. But you are where you are by choice. You came here to experience the wonder of life. You have never stopped being connected to me. The more you communicate with me, the better you will feel. Write, meditate, pray. I hear, I see, I love you.

Habit

ear one, a path that you take for the first time is always most difficult. You can barely tell where you need to walk because it is overgrown with weeds and brush. That first trip is confusing and hard. But to get from here to there the path must be taken. The next time you come to this place you will see more clearly where you have walked before. The day after that it will be clearer still. In time the grass and weeds give way to solid ground and as you repeatedly pass this way the path will grow clearer and wider. If this is true in the world, why would it not be true in your mind. Remember how difficult any new routine is. Yet in a short time, with repeated practice, you don't even have to consciously think about it. You can do other activities while you follow the path. Every time you choose to pay attention to where you are going, you imprint it into your subconscious mind and in a short time you will be as comfortable with it as you are with any other way of life. This works with negative thinking as well. Think about how easily you fall back into your old habits. It is because they have been repeated again and again and their path is clear. It seems so much easier to go down that road again. But that is not going to take you where you say you want to go. Every time you follow the old, familiar, easy path the weeds in the new one have time to spring up and block your way. "Don't go there" is a phrase that is popular these days. Use it to help you remember where you truly want to go. Every time the old ways beckon, don't go there.

Acceptance

You are creating your own troubles. Your attitude toward people and situations is the real problem. I know that is hard to accept but it is true. Here is a way for you to put it to a test. When you go out today, think only love toward everyone you contact. Project all the love in the world on them. Wrap them in a blanket of love, not just human love but holy spirit, God-love. You will see change take place before your very eyes. I suggest you to do this with strangers because you have no ego history with them and it will be easier. In time, you can do it with those closer to you. If you can love truly and completely, your life will change and nothing anyone can do will shake your foundation. Love will be all that matters. The miracle is not arranging the people and situations around you the way you want them, it is knowing that how they are is already perfect. Accept completely, with joy, everything. But do not try to do this alone. Call on me to aid and guide your heart. A little willingness is all that is required.

Mediation And Exercise

*I*s there a problem? You have created it. Now hear this: if you have caused it, you can change it. The external world is not the trouble. Your thoughts about it are what create your stress. And your thoughts are of your own making. Control your mind with meditation and exercise. You will be amazed how effective this can be. Begin today. There is no one holding you back but you. My power will be with you in every effort you make. I am your strength and your comfort. Make your exercise time, time you spend with me. Every repetition, every step, a prayer. I will hear you. Trust me to help. I am not "out there" waiting for you to die so you can be with me. I am here. . .in this paper, in the sunlight and the shadows, in your dreams and your failures. You have me always at your fingertips. Let me guide and strengthen you. Let me in. Your worries cannot defeat you. I am greater than their smallness. Choose joy, choose gratitude, choose grandeur. Choose me. I have already chosen you.

Prayers

I know you often feel like you are praying about the same people and situations over and over. Come to me as many times as necessary, regardless of your own self-judgement. I am happy for your trust in me. I am always with you. I already know your needs and failures. Your prayers help you to know and to put into words your life's turbulence. Until you do, everything is tumbling in your mind. Once you have given your concerns to me, trust me to handle them. Just let it be. Even muddy water will become clear when it remains still. Be still. Rest your troubled heart and mind. You will soon begin to experience some clarity. In the stillness I am there, whispering to your soul.

Example To Others

Others are watching you. Friends and family see how you behave and notice if you are at peace. You can be a lighthouse that guides others through the rocks of their life. But you are only a guide. The light shows the way but it does not come down to the ship and take over even if the captain wants it to. The light can only illuminate the path, the captain must steer his own vessel. I am your light. I will not run your life but I will suggest, inspire, love and guide. You are the captain of your own ship. You must navigate the difficulties of your journey. I will give you a compass, a map and directions but you are at the wheel. This is what you came to learn. This very difficulty is your chosen path. Be ready and willing to reach your goal. You are not alone. I go with you always.

Power Source

My grace and power are around and within you, you just do not use them. Feel yourself energized with my strength. Breath deeply and fill your mind and heart with my power. Transform your will with my guidance. Your pulse and heart throb with the same rhythm that created the stars. Remember who you are. You do not need to meet the world's standards since they are always changing. What you do need to measure is the strength of your character and the depth of your love. You have all the tools you need to build a happy life. But the value of a tool lies only in its use. A hammer will not drive a nail unless you pick it up and position a nail and then bring down the hammer with appropriate force. An electric drill will be of no value unless you plug it in. Pick up your tools and use them. Plug into the power source that will never fail. It's up to you. I will love you no matter what your choice.

Love

My child, how much love you have to give! I see you as a vessel filled to the brim, spilling over. You can give that love to others who thirst for it. Some are so parched that they will wither and die if they are not showered with love. Soak their hearts, drench their dry spirits with the healing waters of your, our love. You do not know how long some of them have waited for a touch, a word, a gesture that will restore their souls. They cannot grow or even live without the soothing, renewing gift of someone's love. Your drops of kindness and attention will lift their dying spirits, and touch their aching hearts. Trust your instincts. I will guide you to those who need your abundant love. Leave it to me to send them your way. You are my hands and heart to a parched and lonely world. Let your love keep flowing. I will fill you with living water over and over.

Changes

*D*ear one, I can and do always speak to you. You, however, do not always choose to listen. Often when you see others who are struggling with a problem, you are amazed that they refuse to accept simple suggestions you give them that could ease their burdens. You cannot understand why they do not see how easily some small changes could help. They are to you as you are to me. I see how you could easily help yourself by making small changes. So much of what you do is only habit. You have already changed many things in your life simply by making yourself willing to begin. Just one day at a time you can do anything! Ask me to help you and I will inspire you beyond your dreams. Remember who you are and why you are here. I love you.

The Puzzle

Do not squander your talents on worthless endeavors. Your treasure lies at your fingertips and yet you fail to pick it up. You worry how others will judge you, but you will never know if you do not give them a chance to see what you offer. If they turn away or ridicule you, that is their choice. It has nothing to do with you. What of the hearts that are longing to know what you know? How will they heal? They are waiting for your gift. Start today to get your house in order. Allow time each morning to speak with me. Still your restless mind and allow my wisdom to pour in. You have no idea how much lies before you. Trust me. Just because you cannot see the "big picture" does not mean it isn't there. Do you always see the puzzle before it is complete? Sometime you have a guide to work from but the actual picture is composed of many pieces. Holding one or even several of them in your hand will not help you. Only when they all finally come together will the beauty become obvious. Each part of your life is like the puzzle pieces, fitting together perfectly. You cannot force them to fit if they are not meant to. You cannot see where each piece belongs before you begin. Only by trying, selecting, moving, arranging the pieces are you able to see what fits. That is life. You have already chosen the picture, you just need to put it together. But while you're at it, have fun.

Be Free

*D*ear one, you say that lately you are out of sorts and feeling down. You are restless and discontent because your soul is ready to change. Begin to free yourself from some of your heaviness: possessions, body weight, meaningless activity. These are the "mud" you feel stuck in. Free yourself from these things and you will wonder how you tolerated the pressure for so long. Give yourself room to spread your spirit wings. Open your heart and make room for grace.

Your Role

Beloved child, remember who you are today. I have told you this before. Also call to mind your purpose, your peace and your power. You are just so caught up in the role you are playing that you think you are the character. That is not true. When the play is over you will once again be who you have always been and are eternally. A being of light and radiance, pure joy, pure love. For now you are immersed in the part you are playing on this stage you call the world. I have not forgotten who you are. I honor your pain and your struggle. Know that you are where you are because it serves your soul's growth. Be not afraid for I am with you always.

Openness

*D*ear one, your openness has enabled me to speak so you can hear me. I speak to everyone, but some close their minds and hearts. Each soul is free to choose, so I will never force myself on anyone. I love it when a few will let me in. My words will flow to any heart. There are many ways to access me - music, art, poetry, dance, service, prayer, meditation, and dreams. All put your spirit in touch with me. We merge and mingle like smoke from two fires, like water drops touching, then separate again, both better than before, more complete, more fulfilled. Each time we unite, we love deeper and stronger. Our awareness of each other is clearer. Like a parent and child who finally start to communicate after years of silence or hostility. My child, I am always connected to you because we are one. I am the light of your flame, the beat of your heart, the sound of your music. Where you are, I am. Open your mind and soul to my transforming love. Listen to my music, look for my light, feel my heart beat. You are loved beyond anything you can understand. We journey together.

Worry

My beloved, your worries will fade like smoke on a breeze. Your gratitude will uplift you and give you wings. There will always be something to be concerned about but if your soul searches for joy, you will balance your mind so that you will not be oppressed with worry. Gratitude lightens your spirit. Worry is like carrying a bag of sand that makes every step a labor. Joy pokes holes in the bag and little by little the load lightens. Soon you will be springing forward, free of your burden of worry or regret. What once slowed you down will be gone. Look for the joy. It is there!

Fear

I am always aware of your needs. The challenges you face are what will make you strong. That is how you to learn to stay calm in the midst of turbulence and focused while tempted by distractions. You already know how, you just choose to forget. This keeps you feeling like a victim and steals away your power. You are afraid of your power. You don't know what will happen if you really use it. If you relinquish your self-defeating, time-wasting behaviors and do what you know you can do, then you think that even more will be required of you. Of course it will. You were meant to do more, be more. This rut is of your own making. This life was selected by you and for you, both as challenge and reward. Like clay given to a potter, you can shape it any way it suits you. What will you create? It is in your hands.

Hostility

The people in your life who bring up your hostility are exactly the way they are supposed to be. I know you don't want to hear that. There will always be others who show a side of themselves that will bring out your irritation, annoyance and judgment. What you do with these feelings will determine who you become. If you argue with, put down or avoid these people are you not becoming more like them? You do not show them a better way to live by joining them in their misery. Wrap love around them. Send prayers to them, hold them in your heart with gentleness. They may not change one bit, but you will. You will see their call for love regardless of appearances. Isn't it when you are the most difficult that you need love more than ever? These people are not in your life by accident. They have been chosen for the gifts they carry. Anyone can be kind to nice people. If you love the unlovable then you are choosing to see me even in my most skillful disguise.

The Camera

Try to find comfort in all that is in your life. Cherish your experiences. Even and especially the "negative" ones. I hope you discover that there are no true negatives, there are only experiences. Your mind is like a camera and you are the one who develops the picture of the world you see. Most people stop processing the film too soon so only a shadowy image emerges. Some close their shutter completely and get no picture at all. Others move the camera too much and life is a blur. There are those too who overexpose their film or get too close or too far away. You see, the world just is. The picture you take of it is up to you. Light, film, focus, skill, composition and development all matter. Any one of these can make the finished product unrecognizable or a work of art. You are the photographer, your mind is the camera. I will help guide and direct your thoughts but you hold the camera. How the final picture turns out is always up to you.

Impatience

I know you get impatient with the process of your growth. Growth is not constant like you want it to be. All life is built on the pulse of being. There is up and down, inhale and exhale, contraction and expansion. Tides flow high and low, there are phases of the moon and the change of seasons. And you are an important part of this plan. Only when you withdraw for a while and allow yourself to feel empty and still can you appreciate the wonder of fulfillment that will come in its appointed time. Nothing in your life is at random, your only job is to choose how you will respond. You have so many opportunities to grow, but this will not happen if you don't struggle some. But you do not need to suffer. If a child is given everything she wants, every time she wants it, she will become lazy and demanding. You already know that and yet you feel upset when you don't get what you want when you want it. You are not here to regress; you came to move forward. I know your heart. You are cherished and protected. You are surrounded with abundance and love beyond your wildest dreams.

Who You Are

*D*o not doubt that my plan for your life is unfolding exactly as it should. Remember who you are. Your spirit is my spirit, your body is made of stardust, your heart beats with the rhythm of the ancient oceans, your thoughts are stirred by timeless memories and your soul sings the songs of the angels. You are my shining star, my golden hope. You are beauty and truth beyond time and space. Do these words frighten or comfort you? Believe always that you are watched over, guided and loved beyond your imagining. Be still. Listen with your heart. Deep within, I am there, whispering my promise to your soul. Peace and clarity be to you, child of my heart. Carry this message: Love is, I am.

Get Real

*Y*our awareness, your sharing, your loving is healing many broken hearts. Sometimes just listening can be as effective as words. Others need to be heard without judgment so they can reclaim their wholeness. You do not have to solve their problems, that is their job. Keep being who you know you are and do not try to be someone else. Others are watching and learning from you. Your special talents are meant to be used. You may gain insight on how to use them more effectively, but do not try to do so in a way that feels "wrong" to your nature. Go with your own flow. Your part is very important and my plan would not be complete without you. Rest in the comfort of my love.

Inertia

What words can stop self-will? What thoughts can heal a mind at war against itself? Once you know your dreams, only action can set you free. Get up, move, walk, clean, drive, work, reach out, talk, write, do anything, but do. Inertia is a powerful force. Once movement begins, you can always change direction if it is necessary. You are here to experience the wonder of this world. Don't worry about getting lost. All paths lead home, home to my heart.

Turmoil

ear one, breathe deeply. Be still. Let my angels whisper to your heart. Release all that troubles you for just a little while and be at peace. The turmoil of the world will fade from your mind and love will enter. Sit with love, with peace, with me. I did not create you for fear. Your concerns are of your own choosing. You can choose otherwise. What are you looking for? You will surely find it. Start today to look for safety, for comfort, for joy. Nothing of the world will bring you peace, peace dwells within. Rest in the wonder of who you really are, divine, joyful, eternal. I will shelter you in the safety of my love.

Response

*D*ear child, song of my heart, allow all your human feelings to be experienced fully. Treasure even the difficult ones. They are testimony to your aliveness. Darkness and light depend on one another to exist. Both are equally important. Continue to behave with dignity and grace. The hard times will pass, as do the happy ones. That is the ebb and flow of life. The clouds retreat, the sun returns. How you respond is the only choice. Fear or love. Choose which you will cling to. Tomorrow will come no matter which choice you make today. But remember your choices shape your life and all tomorrows. Choose life, choose love, choose joy and you choose me.

Goals

I know you carry many worries in your mind. But if you clearly think about it most of them are the same this year as last year. I will inspire you and open doors and put people you need in your life. Nothing you feel worried about will be accomplished while complaining. That will only keep you stuck. Of course, it is not necessary that you do anything. These goals are of your own making. I will love you and cherish you without conditions, without accomplishments, without completions. You are already perfect, whole and complete. Your soul is radiant, joyful and free. If you can understand this one point, then you will walk your path more lightly, attend to your tasks more reverently, accept your burdens more graciously. You are already home in my heart. Each act you perform is sacred, each word you speak is holy, each thought you have is eternal. Your love is blessing the world.

Rebellion

*M*y wonderful child, you are in rebellion. Deep within your mind you resist, you dig in your heels, you want no one, even your higher self, to tell you what to do. You must coax that small, frightened child to walk with you, to take your hand and trust you not to hurt her. You are to that inner child, as I am to you. It has taken some time for you to let me lead you. Your rational mind tells you this is only your imagination talking. Well, I am your imagination, your dreams, your hopes. I am everything, within and without. I am that goal you long for and also the fear of success. There is no place to turn where I am not. It is completely your choice. There is no "wrong" path. There are only easy and difficult ones. Just remember the path that at first seems easiest may hold difficulty further ahead. The obviously harder path could eventually lead you to a smoother journey. What is worthwhile is rarely easy. Every road has problems to overcome. You are the director of this trip. Don't go around in circles because you refuse to follow directions. Don't take the longer, rougher road because you resent having to look at the map that is in your hand. This is your journey and your choice, but you say you want to go north and you continue to drive in every other direction and then double back to the place you began. Only your vehicle is now needing repairs and running out of gas. Often you don't quite get all the way back to your starting point so your goal is even farther away than before. Start now, this moment to dedicate yourself to your dreams. If anything tempts you to change direction, keep your destination clear in your mind. I am with you always, loving you no matter where you are heading, treasuring you beyond your ability to understand. You are light and peace and hope. You are perfect if you never move from the spot you now stand. You are home in my heart forever.

Awareness

*D*ear one, your day is blessed. I know you fret about getting everything done. All the "things" you have to do will eventually be completed or forgotten. Look back on old lists. Remember how important each thing seemed. Now you wonder why it was even on the list. This golden day is yours to be at peace. Be outside a little while and breathe in the fragrance of the air. Look at my beautiful world. You will still have time for your truly necessary jobs. Remember you are here to experience the unbelievable wonder of life. Don't throw away an instant of joy. Cherish every action. Look with love on watering plants, making the bed, reading the book. Whatever you are doing, do it completely, eagerly, attentively. Embrace every moment. Bring yourself to the event with the awareness of a child. You are fulfilling your destiny in every instant that you are fully present to your life. Focus and enjoy.

Lists

My child, you are in control of your time. Remember to do first what you wish to do least. After that the rest is easy. When you look at your "to do" list decide what you are avoiding and just do it. Also remember to ask yourself if doing it gets you closer to your goal. Maybe you can just scratch off something. Of course, I hope you always remember that your ultimate goal is me and that our time together will never be scratched. This exchange is the focus of your soul. All else are the body's dreams. You are beautiful, perfect and eternal. I treasure you and our time together.

Dance

My dear one, your world is of your making. You draw to yourself the people and circumstances you need. Never doubt your part in this dance. We are partners, you and I, as is everyone. Some are not yet ready to hear the melody, to practice the steps, to flow with the rhythm and the energy of the music. You have been waiting for the courage, the right song and a willing partner. May I have this dance?

Perfection

*Y*our very life is magical and the perfection of your soul is poetry. Your spirit is so beautiful that if you were to experience the full radiance of your true self, your mind could not contain it. That is why you need to only have glimpses of your glory now and then. Believe this - your path is not at random.

Recognition

My beloved child, how beautiful your soul is. It is as radiant as a star. It shines its light on the lives of others and helps them see a better way. You have a joyful, gentle spirit that helps other hearts sing. Allow your love to continue blessing the world. You are not here by accident, you are here by choice. Where you walk is holy ground because you are me in another form. All those you encounter, regardless of how they seem, are also filled with me. When everyone remembers who they really are, the world will explode with joy. Until then those of you who know who you are can help others transcend appearances. Don't get caught up in the masquerade. I will always help you remember who you are.

Goodness

Go about your day with awareness. Consciously seek out the goodness in others and their gratitude will bless you back. Then the blessing will radiate out to the world and so continue as souls touch and bless and heal each other. Like the ripples in a pond your impact extends far beyond your point of contact. No action that you take goes unnoticed. It always has an effect. You do not always know what that is but please understand that your very movement through the world touches all things. Therefore, to the best of your ability, choose lovingly the words and actions of this day. If you need help, just think of me and all my power will rush to your side and bless your intentions. I am your best friend, your deepest desire, the longing of your heart. I will never leave you. Open yourself to my love.

Gifts

*B*eloved, remember you are the creator of your experiences. Life happens, but your response to life is up to you. There is always a gift contained in every problem. You have brought the problem into your life because you need the gift it brings. Think about past difficulties and remember what growth came to you only because you had to deal with the problem. Trust life, trust yourself, trust me. You cannot fail, you can only be a little later to arrive. But I will always be here cheering you on, holding your hand, lighting your way. I am the finish line, the trophy that you seek, the gold medal, the blue ribbon, the first prize. And all who are in the race will win. You and all the world will make it safely home.

Shine

Let your heart open to my wisdom minute-by-minute. You will know what to do and say at the time you need it. I could answer all your questions in advance but your mind could not contain all the answers. Just remember, the details are not the point, it's your attitude that matters. You choose the world you see. You decide how you will value your life. You have tremendous power and you will become what you believe yourself to be. You are a bringer of light, so don't forget to shine.

Effort

My child, your love and concern for others is beautiful. You give of yourself so freely. Remember to give back to yourself just as generously. Don't let yourself down with laziness, excuses or lack of planning. Trust yourself to do the next best thing. Get up, exercise, move before you are unable to do so. You still have time to get your act together. Your age is just the excuse you use today to be lazy. If you truly want your body to be healthy and fit you must put some effort into it. Muscle tone comes only with muscle use. Remember seeing a cast come off someone's leg or arm and how wasted and weak the muscles were. That will happen anywhere muscles are not used. You were made to move, dance, run, play. Be active! Get up; get going! I'm there beside you as you dig in your garden, clean your house, as you walk in the park. I encourage you, honor you, love you. I want you to do the same.

Perception

*D*ear, dear child, can you truly feel my embrace? I know you are striving for greater connection with me. I am here within your thoughts and surrounding your being. There is nowhere when I am not enfolding you with my grace, filling you with my love, offering you my peace, showing you your possibilities. How you respond to these gifts is your choice. You make your life wonderful or terrible because of what you choose and how you perceive. You give it all meaning! How many do not understand this simple premise? Help spread the word. Your life is yours to make of it anything you want. Be aware, look around, simplify, create, delight in it all. You are a shining star, clear and bright in the evening sky, a glistening dew drop cupped in an open flower, a crystal snow flake dancing on a winter wind, a candle flame, burning with the fire that never dies. You are all this and more, as is all the world. No one is more or less, greater or smaller. You are all one, like the notes in a symphony. Each depends on all the others to make the perfection, the beauty complete. You are all needed by each other. I am playing the song. Listen for your music. Your soul remembers the tune. Sing along with me. My melody is sweet. My song is you.

Depth

Beloved, the word for today is stillness. How quiet can you be? Not just externally, but in your mind. Go about your day as planned but try to enter into the peace of inner stillness. Like a deep sea diver who does not notice the wind or the waves on the surface of the sea. He is deep in the quiet and peace of the ocean. Be deep in your heart with me. No matter what disturbance rocks the surface of your mind, you are safe in the depth of my love.

Ella Jankowiak

Blessings

Child, blessings are there for everyone but some do not know how to recognize them. Every experience is an opportunity to see light but many choose to look only at the darkness. There are good and bad sides to everything. You are where you are today because of decisions you have made. The minute you change how you look at the world, the world will change. You can choose to see that regardless of external appearances, all is well. Believe!

Reception

*D*ear one, thank you for tuning in. The Grace Station is on the air for everyone. But not all choose to turn the dial away from fear, anger, worry, impatience and guilt. Those stations broadcast louder. You have to search the dial to find grace and then put your ear down close to the radio. You need to tune out the distractions around you and really concentrate on my program. Sometimes you even have to move the radio itself in a different direction so the signal will be clearer. But once you find it and adjust the dial and volume, you will hear the message that is meant for you. Your soul is a receiver. Your program is being broadcast and once you are aligned with the signal your reception will be loud and clear. It is worth the time and effort to tune in. The message is your beacon. Like a tower in the darkness, it will lead you home.

Disguise

Dear one, your life is in your hands which are also mine. Your choices cannot be anything other than my will. You already know your path, your chosen goal. But if you do not follow the road you say you want to travel, that choice is all right too. Just remember, you are doing the choosing. I do not stop your progress or push you along. Your will is strong; your "won't" is also. What is it you really want? Every day, hour, minute, second you get to choose again. Who do you want to be? What fun! What adventure! Like children playing dress up. Each time you get to decide who you want to be today. Be daring, be bold! Throw yourself into the masquerade. This is what you came here for. Just remember it is only a game and your soul never changes. It is pure love, it is me. You choose your hiding place today just like everyone else. Most do not recognize it as a game of hide-and-seek, but I always know exactly who you are. Just like a parent knows their child no matter how hard they try to disguise themselves. I know and love you all. You walk together, hand in hand, coming home to me.

The Game

*D*ear child of my heart, the situations in your life that cause you the most distress are supposed to be there so you can grow. You do not grow in spite of them, you grow because of them. You have drawn them to you for that very purpose. Soon, you will have no need of them because you will have deeply and truly remembered who you are. But know that bliss is not your goal, you only think it is. You have experienced bliss before yet have chosen to play the game again. Think about how players of any game can finish as winners or losers and still sign up to do it all again. It's the love of the game that calls them to play. Yet each and every time they agonize, suffer, rejoice, cheer and struggle to do it better this time. And when it's over - win or lose - in a short time they are back yearning for the challenge of another game. You are here to enjoy it. Win or lose, we are only playing. Your turn....

Virtual Reality

*A*ll is well. There are many choices - not right or wrong, only different, and each will have a thousand other ripple effects that cause you to make other choices and on and on. The only concern you need have is if this choice is a loving one. Does it come from fear or love? If it is hard to tell the difference then you probably need a clearer mind to guide you. Talk to someone whose wisdom you respect. Help is on the way. The cavalry is coming. Just like in the old western movies, at what appears to be the last minute, the heroine is rescued. Only you wrote the script, cast the characters, furnished the set and are directing everything. You just do not remember. You are lost in the movie and think it is real. It is not. Trust love to guide your heart. Relax and know that it is only another wonderful drama you have created. While watching the show remember it is only that, a lifelike, virtual reality trip. At any time you can stop or turn away. You bought your ticket on purpose to have exactly this experience. Sit back, relax and enjoy the show.

Opposites

ou are here to experience life. For that you need to have both "good" and "bad" so you get the entire flavor. Everything has it's opposite. It must, so that it can be appreciated. Remember the quote, "Darkness is as important as light. You must have both to understand the difference." Try to embrace everything because everything is a gift to treasure. Stop judging. Live in the moment. You will be amazed how beautiful the world will shine after the storm has passed. The sunshine awaits you. Just do not drag the clouds along with you or you will be forever in darkness. I am right here. Lay your worries and your fears at my feet. Trust me and you will know peace.

Problems

*W*ho among you has no fear? At times money problems are manifested so that other concerns do not have to be dealt with or health problems keep relationships at bay. There is perfection in the process, growth in the struggle, awareness in the lack. These problems are not at random. The exact lessons that are needed have been selected by the student and the teacher. Your job is not to fix the problem for others. This is their class work and homework. As a friend you should offer comfort and insight but you cannot give them their solutions. They must work through the problem at their own soul's level of learning. Be there for them to lean on but they must stand or fall on their own. There are no failing grades in this school, only awareness, balance and experience. It is all beauty and perfection. Trust me, one day you will understand. The difficult tasks are given to those most able to solve them. These are my honor roll students, destined to succeed. Thank you for caring and cheering them on.

The Big Picture

Beloved, I know how much you care about others. Imagine how much I do, too. There is a plan at work. Often what appears on the surface is disturbing. Yet deep within, other necessary things are taking place. You do not, can not, see the big picture. Like a fly on a movie screen, you are only getting a flickering light and think you see. Believe me, although things seem grim, all is well. Trust the process. You often see people who are impatient, arrogant and fearful and you want them to believe and change and grow. Right now, right here, you need to do that too. You are impatient (that things aren't moving fast enough), arrogant (you are telling me how to do my job), and fearful (that needs won't be met). The external situation is only a stage that helps the inner work unfold. The soul is the thing that is being shaped, polished, and transformed into a treasure far beyond this world's gold. The process can sometimes be very distressing. But the spirit knows its goal. The easy road is not always the best one. Think about how human growth and learning take place. A baby that is always carried will never develop the muscles to walk. Then the actual walking requires standing, holding on, balancing, risking, falling, struggling to stand again, over and over. If all that difficulty never took place, what then? A helpless, weak, dependent child would always exist.

You can easily understand this concept. Try to apply it to the growth of the soul. The baby learning to walk does not conceive the big picture, nor can you really grasp your soul's needs. One day you will understand. In the meantime, enjoy and trust the process. I am always here to comfort and hold your hand. Beloved, lean on me.

A Life

How important one day can be. It is a world, a lifetime unto itself. When you awake, you begin as an infant, sleepy and hungry, slowly gaining strength and awareness. Then you become as a child, energetic, optimistic and eager. Later as an adult, you plan and work, doing your best. Afterward, at the end, you rest and reflect, looking back on the events you experienced, then close your eyes and sleep. This is how you build a day and build a life, one day at a time.

Healthy Diet

*D*ear one, the ideal weight you strive for is not the issue. Weight is often bound to body image and is a matter of fashion. The fashion of the time is usually unnatural. When most low-income people worked outdoors, it was fashionable to have very fair skin. When people find food hard to come by it is desirable to be heavy. This just proves to others that you are financially successful. Your struggle is really with personal integrity. At the moment you find yourself being drawn to your addiction, it is primary that you be aware. Awareness allows you choice. Of course to be unaware is also a choice. It gives you permission (in your mind) to indulge without care. Only after your "trance" do you regret your actions. Now, at that instant of aware choice you will sometimes say "Who cares?" and indulge. But it is important to remember that you care and so do I. Not if you are fat or thin, but that you are true to your life, true to yourself. That is the moment of honor, of integrity and victory. You have a choice every day to drink alcohol, smoke cigarettes, spend money foolishly, steal, lie, gamble or eat poorly. Just for today, stop, think and make your choice based on what you know is true. Choose life, choose strength, choose me.

Enthusiasm

My beautiful child, your enthusiasm for your life is wonderful. You choose joy and love whenever you can and you are making your life happy because of it. Few understand this. You are both the giver and the receiver of your joy. Just keep remembering happiness in the midst of routine jobs, love while engaged in distasteful tasks, forgiveness while dealing with difficult people and above all, remember me. My love is always here to call on when yours is running low. I will never, ever leave you! Remember me!

Connection

Child of my heart, remember that everyone is part of the whole. All are connected. I know it is difficult to understand. Some are my hands, my eyes or my ears. Others are less visible but no less important. Is the heel of your foot not important? Your elbow? Your kidneys? All parts depend on others to function as intended and I love you all. But sometimes the hands must minister to the eyes, the ears hear to heal the heart. All work together for the good of the whole. You are wondrously created - - you the individual and you the whole of creation. Nothing happens that goes unnoticed. At times some things may seem horrible but there is a plan you cannot understand. Please trust the process that will bring the world to peace. You will not fail unless you allow despair to overcome you. The world will go on. Nothing is greater than love.

Don't Miss It

*Y*ou are growing and changing exactly as you need to. Your worries are unnecessary. All things, all things are unfolding as planned. Relax more into your experience of this life. Live it with all your heart, and don't worry. Tension, worry and resentment have never changed a thing except to reduce the joy of the worrier. Have faith. You are in my care. I will never leave you and you can never leave me. We are a part of each other, connected eternally. There is no circumstance or place that will separate us. It is impossible. Deep within you I reside and when your body finally falls away, your spirit and mine will burst forth together, blended and free, joyful and complete. There is nothing to fear except that you miss the opportunity to truly live the life you have been given. Play, laugh, love, risk, trust, give, enjoy. All is well. I love us.

Relax

Child, be gentle with yourself. You do not have to carry the weight of the world. You will tire quickly if you do. Relax and let me be God. You do not need to manage anyone but yourself. Do what you really want to do. The world, the people, the events are in my care. Your "job" is to enjoy your life in spite of what others do. I will help you if you let me. Give your fear and worries to me and I will exchange them for peace. Be as kind to yourself as you are to others. I am always here. Call on my love and I will give you rest.

Loss

There is no loss of any kind. You and everyone share in all things. Another's gain is your gain too. It is only those who do not know this who feel loss. The time for needing to trust blindly is almost over. Soon the world will make a great leap forward in consciousness. Until then, continue to teach love to everyone who comes into your circle of influence. I am watching and guiding all of you, my one and only love.

The Answer

Beloved, thank you for your love. So many do not remember me, especially when rushed or worried. I am here. I do hear and answer. Turn your heart and mind to me in the midst of your distress. Love is the answer to every question, every worry, every sorrow. There is no tomorrow, there is only now, this instant. Yesterday does not exist except in your mind. There is only this remarkable, wonderful, magical, powerful now. Stay conscious of now. This is where life is lived. Smell the sweet air, feel the warm clothes, hear the soft music, taste the rich flavors, see the magnificent sights that surround you. You are blessed beyond your imagining. All your regrets and worries do not exist. You are making them up. Now, now is the answer. Love now. Love your life, your family, your world. Tomorrow never comes. I love you now.

Participation

Your gifts are given so you may help others. The way will open to you as you step out in faith and risk. Remember other times when you have done this. Sometimes you succeeded in your goal, sometimes you did not but always, always, you grew, you learned, you felt alive and vital. That is what life is for, to participate, to be involved, to matter. It is the very stuff of life. You will experience what you came here for. Always I will be with you to guide, comfort and inspire your heart, mind and soul. I love you.

Closeness

I know you long for a closer contact with me. Your closeness is never the question. Your awareness of it is the only issue. I am the beat of your heart, the breath of your lungs, the flow of your blood. I infuse you with my spirit. Turn your thoughts to the center of your being. I am there. You only need to remember. I cannot hold you any closer to my heart and you cannot keep me out of yours. You only can forget that I am there and believe you are alone. You are not. You are never, ever without me.

Dreams

Today begin to allow yourself to do what it is you say you want to do to make your dreams come true. Do it first. Do not distract yourself with meaningless activities. You say you want to exercise, write, learn, create. Do you think that you accomplish any of that while watching television? Your time is under your control. You always choose what to do. Shopping, cleaning, T.V. viewing, reading, talking on the phone are all fine in moderation but I tell you this, you can spend your whole life just doing those things. Your tasks will expand to fill the hours of your days until your dreams slowly die. Is that what you want? I will love you anyway. There is no right or wrong, only your experience. You can choose safety or risk, mundane or magnificent, ordinary or outstanding. You already know how it feels to accomplish goals you have set for yourself. Don't stop now. Many hearts will be touched by your efforts. They are waiting, longing for what only you can offer. I will help you, you will help me. How else will others learn of my love? Oh, child, you are on holy ground. A blessed path is what you walk. Do not resist, move on. I wait with open, welcome arms.

Treasure

Child, you are a blessing. Your joy shines. Do not allow the trials of the world to dim your love-light. No one can change your attitude unless you allow it. Think about how your peace and love has enhanced your life. It is a gift to yourself. Embrace it. You find your happiness because you expect to. Life is a treasure hunt and the treasure is in the joyful hunting. And as you hunt you become the treasure that you seek, golden, radiant, shining. Never give up. You are already the winner.

Pain

Beloved, I know you cannot understand why painful experiences happen. They are beyond your human comprehension but please believe me, they are part of the plan, a necessary ingredient. Hold on to this truth. One day you will be amazed by how all the puzzle pieces fit together. Do you remember when you first found out about sex? You were horrified that such a thing could be done, never mind that it could be enjoyed. That is how it is with the "horrible" things that happen. Your child mind cannot entertain how or why it is necessary. One day you will see that it is perfect. In the meantime, enjoy the life you have and remember that an "easy" life is not always the best. Growth is often painful and messy, like birth. Trust me. I will not let you down.

A Fish In Water

*Y*ou are immersed in my presence like a fish is in water. You breath me, you move within me. You are contained within me. But like the fish, you don't realize this. Only when you think I am not there, when you are on "dry land" do you gasp for my presence. But there is no place that I am not. In every place and every situation and in every person I am there.

Just Do It

*B*e still. Quiet your mind. Spend a few of the minutes of your morning going within. This writing is good but if you write what I say and then rush around as if it doesn't apply to you, what good is it? How many times are you frustrated when your advice to others is ignored? They ask you what to do, you tell them and they continue on as if you had never spoken. My child, this one thing will change your experience of your today's. Five minutes. Is that too long to sink beneath the doing and experience just being? You are not alone, I go there with you. I will introduce you to your soul.

Rebirth

Child of my heart - I am so grateful for you. Through your eyes I can see the beauty, through your hands I can touch another, through your prayers I can bless the world. You are my divine agent, my spokesman, my holy ambassador. Do not take lightly your assignment. It is your highest calling, your grandest moment. Through you and through all others who know my grace I come again into the world. You are the channel for my birth.

Birthday

The anniversary of the day of your birth is a celebration. Just remember to celebrate every day. Life is an adventure. Love, sorrow, joy, tears, tastes, textures, sights, laughter, warmth, longing, comfort are all full of wonder - "wonder full". Each day is a birthday gift. If you thought you would never have tomorrow, how would you experience today? What choices would you make? What would you do differently? Think on this and know that one day this adventure will be over. I say this not to fill your heart with dread, but with appreciation. Now, this instant, is your grandest gift. Don't throw it away or take it for granted. It is rich and full and priceless and it is yours. Happy Birthday!

Recipe

ou are beginning to see beyond the illusion. All external things only reflect back to you your internal drama. Do you feel like a victim? Then you will find situations that will confirm those feelings. If you feel blessed, joyful and grateful you will be able to sustain those internal feelings by finding ways to validate them. You are in charge of your life. The "stuff" of your life is merely the ingredients. You can bake a beautiful cake or create garbage. How will you choose to live? It is up to you but you are not alone. I am real, I am able, I am here -- here now, ready to help you with your recipe. Will you enjoy the heat or run from the kitchen? Either way you are still my beloved, finding your way home to me. The best recipe of all is "I love you".

This Moment

You are exceedingly blessed, as is everyone. Most do not realize this. To discover it you must stay in the moment with gratitude. That opens your eyes, softens your heart and clears your mind. How can you worry when your gratitude blesses everything? All is exactly as it should be. This moment is perfect. Don't miss it by giving it away to yesterday or tomorrow. Look around you. Sense the wonder of simply being. That is what you are here for. Put your whole awareness into this moment. This time will never come again. This is your treasure, this golden, shining now. Cherish it with all your heart just as I do you.

Drop In The Bucket

*D*ear one, all is exactly as it should be. Do not judge your success by external appearances. You are doing inner work, preparing your soul for greatness. Do you think you can fail when I am guiding and energizing you? You can refuse to participate by delay, distraction and resistance, but that is not failure, that is choice. And that is only motivated by fear. You have nothing to fear. Will you have critics? Of course. How can anyone not? Your actions can not depend on your critics, you must be motivated by love. You need and want to help others. This is what you were meant to do and you are ready. This is one more drop in a bucket that is about to overflow. Which drop is the one that makes the difference? The consciousness of mankind is about to make a great leap forward. Trust the process. Enjoy every moment. You are not alone. My angels surround you.

The World Can Wait

Your confusion and indecision can be a distraction to keep you from moving ahead with your goals. Your future is in my hands. Just try to remember to ask for my guidance when you must decide. My wisdom will be there even before you ask. There will be a *knowing*, a *peace* surrounding the direction you take. Some choices are very difficult and there seems no way to find a peaceful answer, but there is always a way. Your mind may be filled with conflict but your soul will be at peace. The way past the endless distractions of your thoughts is found in stillness and silence. Simply sit. Turn off all the electronic noise, push aside the chatter of your mind and turn deep within. You will find peace waiting there. The busyness of the world can wait a while. You will accomplish more by spending ten minutes in conscious contact with me than by hours of frantic working. What is it you are striving for? Accomplishment, admiration, approval, money? These are your ego's goals. Remember who you really are, a beautiful, eternal, perfect, shining spirit who just needs the comfort of home. Come rest in my open arms a few brief moments. Let me refresh your soul. All is well. The world can wait. In the stillness let me fill you with my love.

Soul Print

Every person you talk to will be affected by you just as you are by them. Everyone leaves a soul print. Just remember who you are (a child of mine) and that they are just like you. Enjoy your interaction. Do not try to impress them with your wisdom, just let them know you understand how hard it is for them. It was also hard for you. It still is. If you connect on that level, you will really connect. I am with you, whispering to your heart.

Currency Of Life

*D*ear one, today is yours. You may use the minutes of it anyway you choose, but you cannot save any for tomorrow. How would you spend your money if you knew it would be gone the next day? Would you let it slip away because you knew it would be replaced at dawn? Would you spend it on meaningless things that would clutter your life? Would you give it away? Or would you purchase things of value that you could treasure more as time goes by. The minutes of your days are the currency of your life. You will probably do all the things I mentioned at some time, but with awareness comes choice. You will start to choose more carefully when you understand that how you live today will create both your yesterdays and your tomorrows. That is because it is always today, now, this instant. Turn to me when you're unsure. Let me be your "financial planner." I promise you a good return on your investment. I have only your "interest" at heart.

Drive

Gratitude blesses your life and everyone around you. If you always choose love, that creates a life of joy. You are asking how to proceed with a certain project. You know that the only way to move, in any direction, is to move. Right now you are sitting still. If you are the driver of a car, turning the steering wheel while the car is parked will not take you toward your destination. In fact it takes more effort to turn the wheel while standing still. Once in motion, only the slightest touch is required to correct your direction. Even if you must drive around in circles for a while, or double back and retrace your path, you are still moving. And once you start to move your destination will become reachable. Maps may be required to find your way in unfamiliar territory. Often you may think you are lost, but soon a sign will appear and you will relax because you know you took the right road. You will see new vistas and travel many beautiful places, but first you must get in the car, have a tank full of gas and a destination in mind. Then you need to start the engine and go. No map, no directions will be of value if you never leave the driveway. Nothing is holding you back but your fear, and that is your own creation. It is keeping your foot on the brake. The journey is the reward. I travel beside you. Let's go!

Tug Of War

Your soul is so open and willing to receive. Your mind, however wants to rush and disbelieve. Which one will win the tug-of-war? How many mornings will you fail to be still a few precious minutes? I am always ready to soothe your tattered spirit, to hold you warm and safe against my heart. Just quiet your mind, listen deeply and believe in the process. I am here, I am real, I am your answer before you ask, your light in the darkness. Come to me. This instant is the world's most precious gift. This instant is the compass that will guide you home. You and I, in this instant, heal the world.

Loving Yourself

*Y*ou need to be as gentle with yourself as you are with others. Your life is rich and full but you still must remember to rest and play. Also to exercise and eat wisely. These reminders are things you already know. Just cherish yourself. You will be of no help to others if you do not care for yourself. Let your love flow in your own direction. I will help you if you let me. Every moment offers you choices. Choose well. I stand by your side loving you always.

Victory

The power you have is far beyond what you have allowed yourself to experience. You can do what you have decided to do. You choose minute-to-minute. Small choices, not great triumphs, will be the key. Every time you turn away from temptation, refuse to be distracted, and reach for your best self, you win. Every victory will give you strength and confidence for the next. My grace aids you now, it always has, and always will. I am not far away. I am here giving you ideas and inspiration. You are not in this alone.

Conflict

You ask for my blessings on the troubled world. I tell you the world is already blessed. The problem is not the pain and strife, it is the inability to see past the problems to the wonder. The hard times are what create strength and growth. What if all was perfect? No pain, no struggle? Then there would be no need for courage, generosity, and character, no need for comfort and compassion. Without conflict, peace would have no meaning. There is a plan. There is. Believe!

Light

The grandest accomplishment you can ever have is to share your joy, love and peace with another soul. You are a shining light to many still in darkness. Let yourself shine. Be a beacon. When night is darkest for others, that is when your light is brightest. Even the smallest spark can bring them hope and direction. I will keep your love light protected from the storms. Just know that my arms surround you always. Shine on!

One At A Time

I love you. You are my heart, my voice, my hands. You can change the world for me. Live my words: peace, joy, acceptance, forgiveness, love. Like the child throwing starfish back into the sea; when told he could not save them all, he responded that he could save this one. That is how the world will be saved, one soul at a time. You can not do everything but you can do something. Pass it on. I am here, I am real. You cannot fail.

Remember

Remember I am with you. I walk beside you in the sunshine, I dwell within as you go about your day, I bless you as you fall asleep. There is no thought or deed that you need to hide from me. You are on holy ground, in a sacred space, as is everyone. Often under the pressures of the world, you can forget. You worry, fret, rush and cry when you could be dancing, laughing and loving your existence. It was for you that the world was made, for you that the stars shine, for you that the angels sing. When you enjoy your life, it becomes a gift you give yourself.

Your Body

My dear one, you are so wonderful, but often you do not see your own glory. You are made of the stars and the heavens. You are as luminous and bright as the sun. Your laughter and joy heals broken spirits. You are beautiful beyond your ability to understand. You are, and always will be, perfect. That is your soul. Your body is another story. You must take care of it just as you would any vehicle that you use. That is exactly what it is, a vehicle for your shining spirit. If you let your car sit idle, the tires would dry rot, the engine would not be lubricated, the oil would leak out. Cars were made to be driven, to be useful and help you do the things you want to do. And so is your body. It is meant to move, to delight in activity. Muscles need exercise. Your engine needs good fuel to keep going. Take the car out for a spin. Yes, you might have an accident but sitting in a garage is not what cars are made for. If you do not use it, you may as well not have it. Of course, as always, the choice is yours. I will love you and love you and love you, moving or sitting, driving or parked. But you came here to experience life, to delight in its possibilities. You are the driver, not the vehicle, but without it you cannot get where you say you want to go. Now go get a tune-up and take a drive. The world awaits you.

Spirit

Nothing in this world can diminish your spirit unless you give it the power to do so. Anger, judgment and blame produce so much negative energy. None of it changes anything but you. Give me all your pain and disappointment and I will replace those emotions with peace. You are not your body, your home or your possessions. You are spirit, energy and love. The physical world is only a way to help you experience the wonder of life. You are an angel on earth, feeling, expressing, touching, loving. All things work for your good. You are safe, you are protected, you are loved. There is no place or situation that is beyond my reach. Relax, trust, enjoy your life. All is well.

Float

ever underestimate the power of surrender. Often it is viewed as failure, but I tell you this, acceptance and surrender can give you the peace that you are searching for. Acceptance does not mean approval and surrender does not mean giving up. It means to stop resisting, stop fighting, and flow. There is a plan to the direction of life but the need to be right, the refusal to understand, is damming the river and blocking the natural path. You are not made for anger, hostility and war. You are where you are for experience, bliss and peace. Lay back upon the water and let the current carry you where you are meant to go. You are still clinging to the shore and expecting to get somewhere. Let go! You will not drown, you will be free. It is only you who are holding you back. It takes far more effort to resist than to flow. Let go, let go!

Stress

*D*ear one, my grace surrounds you. You think you can fall from grace, but you cannot. It is impossible. You are always and forever enfolded in my love. There is nothing you must do, you only have to be. The rules and lists are your own creation. Do you think you will be unloved if you do not buy the right gift, cook the best food, clean the house perfectly? You need do none of these. Those who love you will love you anyway. The stress is in your mind. Relax. Do what your heart leads you to do, do what you love, what you enjoy. That is the best gift you can give your family and yourself. Take your time, experience fully what brings you pleasure. Remember your life is not for rushing, worry and guilt, but love, generosity and peace. I am here to help you remember and treasure each moment. Enjoy the blessing that you already are.

Meditation

*B*e still. Before you begin your busy day, sink deep into the reality of my love. Drop your concerns into the healing pool of my grace and let them go. Watch them disappear from sight. They are gone. All that is here now is perfect. You are perfect. There is no need to change or to fix or to control anything or anyone. Relax, enjoy, laugh, embrace, delight in the wonder of life. You are already whole and holy.

Just For Today

There are many gifts that you have given to others, but you have also gifted yourself. Your choices have helped you and will continue to help you. Experiences many would have run from, you have embraced. You have more power than you realize. Everyone does. You are still learning. But just for today, surrender to the moment. Do not waste your precious now by dwelling in yesterday or tomorrow. Even a minute ago is in the past and a minute from now is in the future. This is the truth. Now and love is all there is. Yesterday, tomorrow, regret and fear are only in your mind. Try to be present to this magical, priceless instant. Live now. Be at peace, all is well. Your job is to take care of your own soul. I am always here to help and inspire you. You are my gift and I am yours. Believe!

Role Model

Live your life with all the passion you have in you. Give your best effort to the task at hand. Do everything as if someone were watching. Someone is. Whatever you do, do with love. Your love blesses all the world. Your thoughts of kindness have a ripple effect. Every good deed, tender gesture, understanding word, and caring intention heals the earth. No act goes unnoticed. Your love is lifting spirits, and setting an example. You are always a role model to someone else. This day is your gift. Enjoy it, use it, treasure it, because it will be gone before you know it. Live consciously so you do not regret its passing. Pay attention. I am.

Focus

*D*ear one, rejoice in every minute. Within the instant is the miracle. Right now contains everything you have ever longed for. It is only by comparing the present to the past or future that you feel lack or fear or worry. Stay focused, be here now. Feel the softness of your clothing, the warmth of the room, the pleasure of reading. The moment you become aware you will find your treasure. Hear, touch, sense, smell, taste this instant. That is the beginning of learning to let go, to relinquish the past and future. Now is the only thing there is. You have heard this before, you will hear it again. You and I exist only now.

Snowflakes

*B*eloved, your peace and joy in the midst of turmoil is wonderful. You know so well that you alone are responsible for your attitude. You bless your own life with your thoughts and actions. You are always in my care. No two snowflakes are alike, and each of my beloveds are individual and unique, known intimately by me. Not one is unnoticed or forgotten. I love all, fully, completely, eternally. Be at peace. All is well.

Fulfill Your Dreams

You are never out of my sight. You have a dream you wish to fulfill and yet you say you don't have time. How many hours have been stolen by television, phone calls, unnecessary errands? You do have enough time to make your dream a reality. What will you wish you had done differently if you realized you had no time left? This is not an idle question. Think on this and make your dream a priority in your life. Only you can make it happen, only you can let it die. What do you want? I will not do this for you. You always get to appointments on time, so make an appointment for your dream. This is the most important appointment you will ever have. I invite you to step out with me on this journey you have postponed for so long. Excitement and fear can feel the same. Don't confuse them. There is nothing to fear with me by your side.

Ella Jankowiak

Inner Strength

Beyond the limit of your senses is a realm of beauty and love that reaches out to your spirit, sending you strength, patience and comfort. You are guided and protected. You are the treasure of angels, connected to a limitless source of divine love. What more could you ever need? Rest and renew yourself. The time approaches for your rebirth, your dream is coming true. Gently turn within and hear the whispers of your soul. It has not forgotten the reason you were born. Listen and remember.

Who Do You Think You Are?

*W*ho do you think you are? How many times have you said or thought those words to yourself or another in righteous indignation? What slight or misunderstanding brought that phrase to your lips or mind? Well, with compassion and love I ask you that very question - - Who do you think you are? You have no idea how important the answer is. If you view yourself as weak, fearful, incompetent and lazy that is exactly what you will be. If your self-image is outgoing, friendly, honest and energetic, so it will be. Most people let their body and emotions decide how they will behave. But I tell you this transforming truth; your spirit can override all existing programming. Plug in to my eternal, internal power. Give yourself a few precious minutes at the beginning of your day to reset your viewpoint, recalibrate your compass. You will become what you believe yourself to be. I will tell you in the stillness of your soul who you really are. You are light and love, you are joy and peace, your strength can move mountains and heal broken hearts. How can you be sad or bored, angry or arrogant when you know your true identity? So I ask you again, with love that knows no ending, my beloved, who do you think you are?

Abundance

illingness to see the possibilities in every situation blesses your life and the lives of those around you. Your abundance, like a cup that overflows, is a blessing to others. Continue to shower my love on everyone you can and I will continue to refill your cup. Remember the smaller the vessel of your need, the quicker it will spill over to bless another. Grace and peace and joy to you, my beloved. You are my helper, my messenger and my friend.

Opportunities

Have you ever noticed how quickly weeds begin to grow in sidewalk cracks and between bricks? Even the slightest opening can be a place for life. A crack in the armor of your ego, a tiny space in the minutes of your day can mean new life. A few moments to practice a new skill, to meditate, to take a walk, or call an old friend can plant a seed in the cement of your illusions. It is up to you to decide what takes root in your pathway. You may choose to watch another television show, eat another cookie or recite your list of complaints to someone willing to listen. Weeds or flowers can be yours. Trash or treasure can fill your time. Use the spaces in your day, the small openings in your awareness wisely. For something *will* fill that void. Only you can decide what will grow in your soul. I will help you learn to tell the flowers from the weeds. In the beginning, when plants are small and fragile, it is hard to know the difference. Usually, by the time you recognize what may be unwanted, the plant is strong and the roots are deep. Now they are more difficult to eliminate. Ask me to help you. In time your knowledge of leaf and soil will grow and you will quickly recognize what you do not wish to have in your garden. But always, you get to decide. There is no right or wrong, only your choice. You can even fill it all in with cement and paint it green and I will still never cease to love you.

Channel Surfing

To what station are you tuned? When you turn on your T.V. or radio do you always have the same channel on and watch the familiar faces and voices over and over? What messages are they sending? Violence, fear, anger, and despair? If you always receive these signals, you will always have the same feelings and you will experience these things as your reality. How can you not feel like a victim if all you perceive is a world that attacks and harms. It has been your choice to view this channel, but other stations are also broadcasting. Sometimes you have to look for them but they are there. Tune in to my channel. I am always on the air. My message is peace, courage, hope and love. Once you have found my signal, don't touch that dial. Stay tuned, another all new program is on the air, one designed just for you.

Wonder

There is power in gratitude. It is a benediction on your day. Gratitude changes your attitude, shifts your point of view, and heals your soul. How blessed are those who keep their hearts open to this grace. If you were to lose your vision, what a wonder sight would be; seeing flowers, a sunset or the faces of a loved one. How about sound? What a miracle the sound of a child's laugh, a bird's song, the whisper of your beloved. What would you exchange for touch? The feel of a summer breeze, a hot shower, a silk shirt, a cool sheet? Each of these, I tell you, is a miracle. You came to experience these amazing things: the taste of a peach, the smell of rain, and the sound of thunder. If you had not been born you would have missed them. Don't miss them because you are busy or worried or tired. This day will not come again. You are here, now. Love every "wonder full" minute.

Listening

*M*y wonderful soul-child, are you listening to me? I do not mean obeying, I mean listening. Perhaps I could say listening 'for' me. I do speak to you, but the constant sounds you surround yourself with keep you from hearing me. Today, just for a little while, let yourself be still. Turn off the electronic noise makers you use to distract your spirit. They are a wall blocking my soft whispers to your soul. There are some things you cannot mute - traffic, the low hum of appliances, the furnace sending warmth into your home, airplanes streaking overhead, sirens and voices from the street. Just turn off what you can and listen. Now what do you hear? Close your eyes. Unfamiliar, distant sounds begin to reach you - - a bird, the faint stir of leaves. They seem new but have always been there. You have just blocked them with your wall of noise. I am everywhere, but you hear me best in silence. Come to me a few quiet moments and let me tell who you really are. You are my hands and heart in this aching world. Touch someone, help them in their pain, and you rise above your own. If you do not know this you will continue to search without finding. You can read books, listen to tapes, go to lectures and meetings, all worthy uses of your time, but a few silent moments everyday with me will tell you more than all the words that man has written? Be still. Breathe. Quiet the chatter in your mind. Sink into the softness of my love and my gentleness. You can now hear what is for you alone. My words are whispering to your soul. Be still and know that I am.

Rest

Beloved, you need rest, exercise and stretching. Walking, yoga, and better nutrition will revitalize you. Give yourself a break. You do not have to mail cards or cook big meals or respond to all requests so that others know you care, they know already. People are watching you. What are you showing them if you exhaust yourself with frantic activity? How does it honor anyone? This year, let your light shine by doing what you really want to do. Be joy-filled, rested, energized, and healthy. You are surrounded with my love. Show the world what that really means. It is peace.

Judgement

Beyond externals, beneath every visible difficulty, within each trial, peace and grace already dwell. It is the inability to accept the moment, and the resistance to what is, that creates your pain. Even as you observe someone in distress, your judgment, your non-acceptance of their plight, fires the energy of pain. Help others where and when you are able. Hold a peaceful place in your heart for them and for yourself. Let them know they are safe with you just as you are with me. All is well. You and all the world are enfolded in my love.

Choice

egin now, today, to make each minute count. Your days can be an amazing testimony of what love can do. Choose not meaningless activity but reflective, deliberate action. Turn within and let your heart decide what really matters. Then be passionate about your decision. Don't be distracted by trivialities. The choices you make will bring you either peace or regret. At the end of each day, each week, what you decide will determine and define your life. If you only choose wisely for a few minutes, it will give you the success your spirit needs to keep going a little while longer. These moments will be the key that unlocks the door to your dreams. Everyone has the same twenty four hours in their day. The choice is yours. I will inspire, direct and comfort you but you must do the footwork. This is your life. I will guide but I will not decide. Remember to love, breathe and pay attention. This moment is perfect, just like you.

Trust

Your trust in me is wonderful. I know how much you are afraid but still you believe. That faith will carry you over every difficulty. I do not remove the problem, I give you the strength to overcome and to transcend the problem. I sow the seeds of the solution. Your faith (sunshine) in the midst of your tears (rain) make the roots go deep and the little hard seed grows into a living, healthy plant. Remember, in the darkest hour, I am still here, listening, guiding and loving all the world.

Appearances

eloved, surrender. What? Everything! Do not have expectations of outcomes and you will not be disappointed. External appearances are meaningless shadows that come and go. Do not decide you are more spiritual because your spouse is faithful or your dog doesn't chew your shoes. Jesus had a life that didn't work out so well on the surface. Do you think you deserve more because you say the right prayers? I do not dispense blessings to some and withhold them from others. Some of the world's most needy are far more spiritual than those with all the trappings of wealth. The peace of God surpasses all understanding. Seek peace in all your choices. Dwell in stillness for a while each day and you will come to know what the peaceful choice is. Do not worry about what the world thinks because that does not matter. What does matter is how much you have chosen to live beyond appearances and give love to even the unlovable. That is where you will find me waiting for you. Then you will truly know who I am.

Magnets

*I*f you can see the wonder and perfection in even the smallest thing, that awareness blesses the whole. Every one who comes to even an instant of clarity brings grace to the world. Like a magnet attracting iron filings, once you draw some bits to you, they carry the magnetic force within them and attract other parts. You have no idea how much even the smallest effort matters. Remember to be what you want to see in your world. I will always be here, guiding and directing your magnetic personality.

Strength

You ask for strength but I tell you that you already have the strength you need. You always have the authority to decide what it is you need to do. What you may fail to see is that you have chosen by default what your ego has told you to be - a victim, helpless in the face of temptation. You believe you are driven to do something and then you behave accordingly. That is not true! It is only what you have decided. You always have the opportunity to choose again! Choose to be healthy, energetic and happy and your self-concept will follow your image of who you are. You will then be much more comfortable in your life. Your true self is spirit and light, laughter and joy, love and wonder. You are my perfect, whole, beloved child, as is everyone. So choose! Choose life, health, and joy. Choose me! I have already chosen you.

Now

You are learning that life is about now. No matter what has happened or is about to happen it is always now. Now is when you make your choice, now is when you have your power, now is when you live your life. And it is always, always now. What happened even a second ago is gone and you have entered a bright, fresh, untarnished now. This instant, this instant, this precious instant. That is life. Do not be at war with tomorrow, be at peace with now. It is not impossible, you only think it is. Give now a chance to create the peace you seek. Do not drag yesterday's regrets or tomorrow's fears into this shining moment. Live it with joy and gratitude. It takes some practice, but it is the key to peace. Honor now.

Cherish Yourself

*B*e as gentle and loving with yourself as you are with others. You need good food, peaceful thoughts, rest and recreation. You are learning, stumbling, falling and then starting over again, like everyone. You are not unique or different. Stay in the moment and bring your joy into it. Do not despair. You are never alone. Rest in me, nourish yourself with my love.

Enjoy The Show

*I*f you knew exactly why difficulties happen there would be no need for faith. It would be like knowing all that is going on behind the scenes of a movie. So much that you do not see is what makes the finished product beautiful. The make-up, casting, rehearsals, retakes, special effects and editing all play their part in the production. If you knew each detail you would not be absorbed in the story line. You would analyze and critique things, or at the least, be disenchanted. You do not need that information now. Just sit back, relax and enjoy the show. The show is the story of your life in which you are perfectly cast. There are no rehearsals. This is it. Action! You will all enjoy the cast party later.

Preparing For The Day

B e still with me awhile. Let my peace wash over your busy mind. Imagine a clear, fresh spring, sparkling and pure. It is flowing through your heart. Any speck of anger, sorrow or worry is flushed out and swept away. Tiny, unnoticed thoughts are cleansed and shining now. These few moments spent preparing your soul for the day are as important as washing and arranging your body. You brush your teeth, fix your hair, and make your external self look and smell appealing. Do not neglect your soul. Your inner light will shine on and connect with others who are searching for a glimmer of love. This is much more important than the body you present to the world. Let your light shine for you are leading others home.

Silence

$\mathcal{B}$ egin your day with meditation. Close your eyes, still your thinking, slow your breathing and just be. Be with the peace beyond doing. Listen deeply to the wisdom of silence. You do not need to be endlessly busy. Even when you "relax" you distract your mind with television, reading, planning and remembering. All these are fine in moderation but not when indulged in continuously. It is like you are on a diet of junk food, always hungry, craving more but never nourished. For a few brief minutes at the start of each golden day, be still and feed your soul. There, in the silence you will find me waiting. I have never left your side. Be still awhile with me.

Attitude

How you experience your life is always up to you. Many people with greater wealth and position are unhappy. They filter their world through an attitude of lack, always wanting more and more of what they do not need. Call forth your day through a filter of abundance, being grateful for everything, grasping for nothing. Create your joy by blessing everything with gratitude. You can discover the buried treasure the world is searching for. It lies deep within each heart. It is love, it is peace, it is me.

Inner Space

e still. Sink into silence. Immerse yourself in the vast inner space of your soul. You are more than the petty, repetitive worries of the world. You want peace, love and grace in your life. My child, you *are* peace, love and grace. To know this, you must be still long enough to experience it. Stop reading, writing, talking, and doing for just a few silent moments. Let the miracle of who you really are find it's way to your heart. Now, in this moment, be still.

Solutions

*Y*our attitude, your view of your life is what blesses it. It is your heart that matters, your love that overflows and brings blessings into your life. Every life lived fully, has struggle, pain, adversity and grief. It is not the external pressures that molds your life, but your reaction to them. Will you run from your trials or become stronger? What is it you are actually afraid of? I do not give you the answers, I give you the ability to discover the solutions. That is true grace, the overcoming of your challenges. I will comfort and sustain you through your darkest hour. Dawn is just a heartbeat away.

You Are The World

$\mathcal{B}$e as willing to embrace the negative situations and people in your life as the beautiful ones. This is where your growth resides. Overcoming challenges is how your learn, and how you evolve. Gratitude in easy times is something that anyone can have, but in times of loss or conflict, that is when it matters. That is what molds your character. I do not mean that you should never be sad or agitated, but do not carry the negativity into the next experience. Let it go. Move forward into the new and shining moment, free of judgment and resentment. You are the creator of your life. Your attitude blesses or curses your day. There is nothing external that can dim your joy unless you give it the power to do so. You do not prove your love for a lost loved one by destroying your own life. Is that how you would want others to behave when you make your transition? You do not win another's love by pointing out their faults and being disgusted by their behavior. Would that make you more lovable? Release your frustration, worry or fear. You cannot be diminished, defeated, or overcome by the world. You are the world. The life you live is held within your hands. Hold it tenderly.

Ownership

*B*egin today to see past the illusion of ownership. Everything belongs to everyone and nothing belongs to anyone. It is all temporary. You are just passing through and all that seems to be yours will one day be given to another. Do not cling with pride to material objects that appear to prove your worth. It is just a game you are playing, moving pieces around a board and delighting in winning. I tell you that you are all winners. Remember that it is a game and you all play willingly. The joy is in the playing.

Giving

D o not confuse giving with having. Since you truly own nothing and there is no loss of any kind, give generously and willingly. Everything will come to you that is required. Remember that the value is in the giving, not the gift. A small token is often as appreciated as a large one, especially when it is unexpected. Gifts can come in many forms: time, empathy, forgiveness, patience, respect and trust. Give as freely as you would receive. You will then know true abundance.

Epilogue

To be continued. This book will never be finished, but now you need to write the next chapter for yourself. My mornings with my journal are a time I treasure. Sometimes days will pass before I feel the stirring that urges me to write an answer to my prayers. But the more I am willing and open, the more it seems to happen. I invite you to be still awhile with your Higher Power, whatever you understand that to be, and *listen*. Listen to your heart, your breath, your soul. The whisper of knowing can only be heard in silence. I wish you joy as you search for buried treasure in the only place it can be found.

Printed in the United States
200788BV00001BA/1-51/A